Addresses
and
Contact
Details

TRIED &
TRUSTED
INDIE PUBLISHING

ISBN: 9781708315757

Tried and Trusted Indie Publishing
www.tatindiepublishing.com.au
triedandtrustedindie@gmail.com

Name:

Address:

Home:

Mobile: Work:

Email: Fax:

Notes:

Name:

Address:

Home:

Mobile: Work:

Email: Fax:

Notes:

Name:

Address:

Home:

Mobile: Work:

Email: Fax:

Notes:

A

Name:
Address:

Home:
Mobile: | Work:
Email: | Fax:
Notes:

Name:
Address:

Home:
Mobile: | Work:
Email: | Fax:
Notes:

Name:
Address:

Home:
Mobile: | Work:
Email: | Fax:
Notes:

Name:

Address:

Home:

Mobile: | Work:

Email: | Fax:

Notes:

Name:

Address:

Home:

Mobile: | Work:

Email: | Fax:

Notes:

Name:

Address:

Home:

Mobile: | Work:

Email: | Fax:

Notes:

A

Name:

Address:

Home:

Mobile: Work:

Email: Fax:

Notes:

Name:

Address:

Home:

Mobile: Work:

Email: Fax:

Notes:

Name:

Address:

Home:

Mobile: Work:

Email: Fax:

Notes:

Name:

Address:

Home:

Mobile: Work:

Email: Fax:

Notes:

Name:

Address:

Home:

Mobile: Work:

Email: Fax:

Notes:

Name:

Address:

Home:

Mobile: Work:

Email: Fax:

Notes:

B

Name:

Address:

Home:

Mobile:	Work:
Email:	Fax:

Notes:

Name:

Address:

Home:

Mobile:	Work:
Email:	Fax:

Notes:

Name:

Address:

Home:

Mobile:	Work:
Email:	Fax:

Notes:

Name:

Address:

Home:

Mobile: | Work:

Email: | Fax:

Notes:

Name:

Address:

Home:

Mobile: | Work:

Email: | Fax:

Notes:

Name:

Address:

Home:

Mobile: | Work:

Email: | Fax:

Notes:

B

Name:

Address:

Home:

Mobile: | Work:

Email: | Fax:

Notes:

Name:

Address:

Home:

Mobile: | Work:

Email: | Fax:

Notes:

Name:

Address:

Home:

Mobile: | Work:

Email: | Fax:

Notes:

Name:

Address:

Home:

Mobile: | Work:

Email: | Fax:

Notes:

Name:

Address:

Home:

Mobile: | Work:

Email: | Fax:

Notes:

Name:

Address:

Home:

Mobile: | Work:

Email: | Fax:

Notes:

e

Name:

Address:

Home:

Mobile:	Work:
Email:	Fax:

Notes:

Name:

Address:

Home:

Mobile:	Work:
Email:	Fax:

Notes:

Name:

Address:

Home:

Mobile:	Work:
Email:	Fax:

Notes:

e

Name:

Address:

Home:

Mobile: Work:

Email: Fax:

Notes:

Name:

Address:

Home:

Mobile: Work:

Email: Fax:

Notes:

Name:

Address:

Home:

Mobile: Work:

Email: Fax:

Notes:

e

Name:

Address:

Home:

Mobile: | Work:

Email: | Fax:

Notes:

Name:

Address:

Home:

Mobile: | Work:

Email: | Fax:

Notes:

Name:

Address:

Home:

Mobile: | Work:

Email: | Fax:

Notes:

Name:

Address:

Home:

Mobile: Work:

Email: Fax:

Notes:

Name:

Address:

Home:

Mobile: Work:

Email: Fax:

Notes:

Name:

Address:

Home:

Mobile: Work:

Email: Fax:

Notes:

D

Name:

Address:

Home:

Mobile: Work:

Email: Fax:

Notes:

Name:

Address:

Home:

Mobile: Work:

Email: Fax:

Notes:

Name:

Address:

Home:

Mobile: Work:

Email: Fax:

Notes:

D

Name:

Address:

Home:

Mobile: Work:

Email: Fax:

Notes:

Name:

Address:

Home:

Mobile: Work:

Email: Fax:

Notes:

Name:

Address:

Home:

Mobile: Work:

Email: Fax:

Notes:

D

Name:

Address:

Home:

| Mobile: | Work: |
| Email: | Fax: |

Notes:

Name:

Address:

Home:

| Mobile: | Work: |
| Email: | Fax: |

Notes:

Name:

Address:

Home:

| Mobile: | Work: |
| Email: | Fax: |

Notes:

Name:

Address:

Home:

Mobile: | Work:

Email: | Fax:

Notes:

Name:

Address:

Home:

Mobile: | Work:

Email: | Fax:

Notes:

Name:

Address:

Home:

Mobile: | Work:

Email: | Fax:

Notes:

E

Name:

Address:

Home:

Mobile:	Work:
Email:	Fax:

Notes:

Name:

Address:

Home:

Mobile:	Work:
Email:	Fax:

Notes:

Name:

Address:

Home:

Mobile:	Work:
Email:	Fax:

Notes:

Name:

Address:

Home:

Mobile: | Work:

Email: | Fax:

Notes:

Name:

Address:

Home:

Mobile: | Work:

Email: | Fax:

Notes:

Name:

Address:

Home:

Mobile: | Work:

Email: | Fax:

Notes:

E

Name:

Address:

Home:

Mobile: | Work:

Email: | Fax:

Notes:

Name:

Address:

Home:

Mobile: | Work:

Email: | Fax:

Notes:

Name:

Address:

Home:

Mobile: | Work:

Email: | Fax:

Notes:

F

Name:

Address:

Home:

Mobile: Work:

Email: Fax:

Notes:

Name:

Address:

Home:

Mobile: Work:

Email: Fax:

Notes:

Name:

Address:

Home:

Mobile: Work:

Email: Fax:

Notes:

F

Name:

Address:

Home:

Mobile: Work:

Email: Fax:

Notes:

Name:

Address:

Home:

Mobile: Work:

Email: Fax:

Notes:

Name:

Address:

Home:

Mobile: Work:

Email: Fax:

Notes:

Name:

Address:

Home:

Mobile: Work:

Email: Fax:

Notes:

Name:

Address:

Home:

Mobile: Work:

Email: Fax:

Notes:

Name:

Address:

Home:

Mobile: Work:

Email: Fax:

Notes:

F

Name:

Address:

Home:

Mobile: Work:

Email: Fax:

Notes:

Name:

Address:

Home:

Mobile: Work:

Email: Fax:

Notes:

Name:

Address:

Home:

Mobile: Work:

Email: Fax:

Notes:

Name:

Address:

Home:

Mobile: | Work:

Email: | Fax:

Notes:

Name:

Address:

Home:

Mobile: | Work:

Email: | Fax:

Notes:

Name:

Address:

Home:

Mobile: | Work:

Email: | Fax:

Notes:

$\mathcal{G}$

Name:

Address:

Home:

Mobile: Work:

Email: Fax:

Notes:

Name:

Address:

Home:

Mobile: Work:

Email: Fax:

Notes:

Name:

Address:

Home:

Mobile: Work:

Email: Fax:

Notes:

Name:

Address:

Home:

Mobile: | Work:

Email: | Fax:

Notes:

Name:

Address:

Home:

Mobile: | Work:

Email: | Fax:

Notes:

Name:

Address:

Home:

Mobile: | Work:

Email: | Fax:

Notes:

G

Name:

Address:

Home:

Mobile: Work:

Email: Fax:

Notes:

Name:

Address:

Home:

Mobile: Work:

Email: Fax:

Notes:

Name:

Address:

Home:

Mobile: Work:

Email: Fax:

Notes:

Name:

Address:

Home:

Mobile: | Work:

Email: | Fax:

Notes:

Name:

Address:

Home:

Mobile: | Work:

Email: | Fax:

Notes:

Name:

Address:

Home:

Mobile: | Work:

Email: | Fax:

Notes:

H

Name:

Address:

Home:

| Mobile: | Work: |
| Email: | Fax: |

Notes:

Name:

Address:

Home:

| Mobile: | Work: |
| Email: | Fax: |

Notes:

Name:

Address:

Home:

| Mobile: | Work: |
| Email: | Fax: |

Notes:

H

Name:

Address:

Home:

Mobile: Work:

Email: Fax:

Notes:

Name:

Address:

Home:

Mobile: Work:

Email: Fax:

Notes:

Name:

Address:

Home:

Mobile: Work:

Email: Fax:

Notes:

H

Name:

Address:

Home:

Mobile: | Work:

Email: | Fax:

Notes:

Name:

Address:

Home:

Mobile: | Work:

Email: | Fax:

Notes:

Name:

Address:

Home:

Mobile: | Work:

Email: | Fax:

Notes:

Name:

Address:

Home:

Mobile: Work:

Email: Fax:

Notes:

Name:

Address:

Home:

Mobile: Work:

Email: Fax:

Notes:

Name:

Address:

Home:

Mobile: Work:

Email: Fax:

Notes:

q

Name:

Address:

Home:

| Mobile: | Work: |
| Email: | Fax: |

Notes:

Name:

Address:

Home:

| Mobile: | Work: |
| Email: | Fax: |

Notes:

Name:

Address:

Home:

| Mobile: | Work: |
| Email: | Fax: |

Notes:

Name:

Address:

Home:

Mobile: Work:

Email: Fax:

Notes:

Name:

Address:

Home:

Mobile: Work:

Email: Fax:

Notes:

Name:

Address:

Home:

Mobile: Work:

Email: Fax:

Notes:

q

Name:

Address:

Home:

Mobile: | Work:

Email: | Fax:

Notes:

Name:

Address:

Home:

Mobile: | Work:

Email: | Fax:

Notes:

Name:

Address:

Home:

Mobile: | Work:

Email: | Fax:

Notes:

Name:

Address:

Home:

Mobile: Work:

Email: Fax:

Notes:

Name:

Address:

Home:

Mobile: Work:

Email: Fax:

Notes:

Name:

Address:

Home:

Mobile: Work:

Email: Fax:

Notes:

J

Name:

Address:

Home:

Mobile: Work:

Email: Fax:

Notes:

Name:

Address:

Home:

Mobile: Work:

Email: Fax:

Notes:

Name:

Address:

Home:

Mobile: Work:

Email: Fax:

Notes:

Name:

Address:

Home:

Mobile: Work:

Email: Fax:

Notes:

Name:

Address:

Home:

Mobile: Work:

Email: Fax:

Notes:

Name:

Address:

Home:

Mobile: Work:

Email: Fax:

Notes:

J

Name:

Address:

Home:

Mobile: Work:

Email: Fax:

Notes:

Name:

Address:

Home:

Mobile: Work:

Email: Fax:

Notes:

Name:

Address:

Home:

Mobile: Work:

Email: Fax:

Notes:

Name:

Address:

Home:

Mobile: Work:

Email: Fax:

Notes:

Name:

Address:

Home:

Mobile: Work:

Email: Fax:

Notes:

Name:

Address:

Home:

Mobile: Work:

Email: Fax:

Notes:

K

Name:

Address:

Home:

Mobile:	Work:
Email:	Fax:

Notes:

Name:

Address:

Home:

Mobile:	Work:
Email:	Fax:

Notes:

Name:

Address:

Home:

Mobile:	Work:
Email:	Fax:

Notes:

K

Name:

Address:

Home:

Mobile: Work:

Email: Fax:

Notes:

Name:

Address:

Home:

Mobile: Work:

Email: Fax:

Notes:

Name:

Address:

Home:

Mobile: Work:

Email: Fax:

Notes:

K

Name:
Address:

Home:
Mobile: | Work:
Email: | Fax:
Notes:

Name:
Address:

Home:
Mobile: | Work:
Email: | Fax:
Notes:

Name:
Address:

Home:
Mobile: | Work:
Email: | Fax:
Notes:

Name:

Address:

Home:

Mobile: | Work:

Email: | Fax:

Notes:

Name:

Address:

Home:

Mobile: | Work:

Email: | Fax:

Notes:

Name:

Address:

Home:

Mobile: | Work:

Email: | Fax:

Notes:

L

Name:

Address:

Home:

Mobile: Work:

Email: Fax:

Notes:

Name:

Address:

Home:

Mobile: Work:

Email: Fax:

Notes:

Name:

Address:

Home:

Mobile: Work:

Email: Fax:

Notes:

Name:

Address:

Home:

Mobile: | Work:

Email: | Fax:

Notes:

Name:

Address:

Home:

Mobile: | Work:

Email: | Fax:

Notes:

Name:

Address:

Home:

Mobile: | Work:

Email: | Fax:

Notes:

L

Name:

Address:

Home:

Mobile:	Work:
Email:	Fax:

Notes:

Name:

Address:

Home:

Mobile:	Work:
Email:	Fax:

Notes:

Name:

Address:

Home:

Mobile:	Work:
Email:	Fax:

Notes:

$\mathcal{M}$

Name:

Address:

Home:

Mobile: Work:

Email: Fax:

Notes:

Name:

Address:

Home:

Mobile: Work:

Email: Fax:

Notes:

Name:

Address:

Home:

Mobile: Work:

Email: Fax:

Notes:

M

Name:

Address:

Home:

Mobile: | Work:

Email: | Fax:

Notes:

Name:

Address:

Home:

Mobile: | Work:

Email: | Fax:

Notes:

Name:

Address:

Home:

Mobile: | Work:

Email: | Fax:

Notes:

Name:

Address:

Home:

Mobile: Work:

Email: Fax:

Notes:

Name:

Address:

Home:

Mobile: Work:

Email: Fax:

Notes:

Name:

Address:

Home:

Mobile: Work:

Email: Fax:

Notes:

𝓜

Name:

Address:

Home:

Mobile: Work:

Email: Fax:

Notes:

Name:

Address:

Home:

Mobile: Work:

Email: Fax:

Notes:

Name:

Address:

Home:

Mobile: Work:

Email: Fax:

Notes:

Name:

Address:

Home:

Mobile: Work:

Email: Fax:

Notes:

Name:

Address:

Home:

Mobile: Work:

Email: Fax:

Notes:

Name:

Address:

Home:

Mobile: Work:

Email: Fax:

Notes:

N

Name:

Address:

Home:

Mobile: | **Work:**

Email: | **Fax:**

Notes:

Name:

Address:

Home:

Mobile: | **Work:**

Email: | **Fax:**

Notes:

Name:

Address:

Home:

Mobile: | **Work:**

Email: | **Fax:**

Notes:

Name:

Address:

Home:

Mobile: Work:

Email: Fax:

Notes:

Name:

Address:

Home:

Mobile: Work:

Email: Fax:

Notes:

Name:

Address:

Home:

Mobile: Work:

Email: Fax:

Notes:

N

Name: _____

Address: _____

_____

Home: _____

Mobile: _____ | **Work:** _____

Email: _____ | **Fax:** _____

Notes: _____

Name: _____

Address: _____

_____

Home: _____

Mobile: _____ | **Work:** _____

Email: _____ | **Fax:** _____

Notes: _____

Name: _____

Address: _____

_____

Home: _____

Mobile: _____ | **Work:** _____

Email: _____ | **Fax:** _____

Notes: _____

Name:

Address:

Home:

Mobile: | Work:

Email: | Fax:

Notes:

Name:

Address:

Home:

Mobile: | Work:

Email: | Fax:

Notes:

Name:

Address:

Home:

Mobile: | Work:

Email: | Fax:

Notes:

O

Name:
Address:

Home:
Mobile: | Work:
Email: | Fax:
Notes:

Name:
Address:

Home:
Mobile: | Work:
Email: | Fax:
Notes:

Name:
Address:

Home:
Mobile: | Work:
Email: | Fax:
Notes:

Name:

Address:

Home:

Mobile: Work:

Email: Fax:

Notes:

Name:

Address:

Home:

Mobile: Work:

Email: Fax:

Notes:

Name:

Address:

Home:

Mobile: Work:

Email: Fax:

Notes:

Name:

Address:

Home:

Mobile: | Work:

Email: | Fax:

Notes:

Name:

Address:

Home:

Mobile: | Work:

Email: | Fax:

Notes:

Name:

Address:

Home:

Mobile: | Work:

Email: | Fax:

Notes:

Name:

Address:

Home:

Mobile: Work:

Email: Fax:

Notes:

Name:

Address:

Home:

Mobile: Work:

Email: Fax:

Notes:

Name:

Address:

Home:

Mobile: Work:

Email: Fax:

Notes:

P

Name:

Address:

Home:

Mobile:	Work:
Email:	Fax:

Notes:

Name:

Address:

Home:

Mobile:	Work:
Email:	Fax:

Notes:

Name:

Address:

Home:

Mobile:	Work:
Email:	Fax:

Notes:

Name:

Address:

Home:

Mobile: Work:

Email: Fax:

Notes:

Name:

Address:

Home:

Mobile: Work:

Email: Fax:

Notes:

Name:

Address:

Home:

Mobile: Work:

Email: Fax:

Notes:

P

Name:

Address:

Home:

Mobile: | Work:

Email: | Fax:

Notes:

Name:

Address:

Home:

Mobile: | Work:

Email: | Fax:

Notes:

Name:

Address:

Home:

Mobile: | Work:

Email: | Fax:

Notes:

Name:

Address:

Home:

Mobile: | Work:

Email: | Fax:

Notes:

Name:

Address:

Home:

Mobile: | Work:

Email: | Fax:

Notes:

Name:

Address:

Home:

Mobile: | Work:

Email: | Fax:

Notes:

Q

Name:

Address:

Home:

Mobile: Work:

Email: Fax:

Notes:

Name:

Address:

Home:

Mobile: Work:

Email: Fax:

Notes:

Name:

Address:

Home:

Mobile: Work:

Email: Fax:

Notes:

Name:

Address:

Home:

Mobile: | Work:

Email: | Fax:

Notes:

Name:

Address:

Home:

Mobile: | Work:

Email: | Fax:

Notes:

Name:

Address:

Home:

Mobile: | Work:

Email: | Fax:

Notes:

Q

Name:

Address:

Home:

| Mobile: | Work: |
| Email: | Fax: |

Notes:

Name:

Address:

Home:

| Mobile: | Work: |
| Email: | Fax: |

Notes:

Name:

Address:

Home:

| Mobile: | Work: |
| Email: | Fax: |

Notes:

R

Name:
Address:

Home:
Mobile: Work:
Email: Fax:
Notes:

Name:
Address:

Home:
Mobile: Work:
Email: Fax:
Notes:

Name:
Address:

Home:
Mobile: Work:
Email: Fax:
Notes:

$\mathcal{R}$

Name:

Address:

Home:

Mobile: | Work:

Email: | Fax:

Notes:

Name:

Address:

Home:

Mobile: | Work:

Email: | Fax:

Notes:

Name:

Address:

Home:

Mobile: | Work:

Email: | Fax:

Notes:

Name:

Address:

Home:

Mobile: Work:

Email: Fax:

Notes:

Name:

Address:

Home:

Mobile: Work:

Email: Fax:

Notes:

Name:

Address:

Home:

Mobile: Work:

Email: Fax:

Notes:

R

Name:

Address:

Home:

Mobile: Work:

Email: Fax:

Notes:

Name:

Address:

Home:

Mobile: Work:

Email: Fax:

Notes:

Name:

Address:

Home:

Mobile: Work:

Email: Fax:

Notes:

Name:

Address:

Home:

Mobile: | Work:

Email: | Fax:

Notes:

Name:

Address:

Home:

Mobile: | Work:

Email: | Fax:

Notes:

Name:

Address:

Home:

Mobile: | Work:

Email: | Fax:

Notes:

$\mathcal{S}$

Name:
Address:

Home:
Mobile: | Work:
Email: | Fax:
Notes:

Name:
Address:

Home:
Mobile: | Work:
Email: | Fax:
Notes:

Name:
Address:

Home:
Mobile: | Work:
Email: | Fax:
Notes:

Name:

Address:

Home:

Mobile: Work:

Email: Fax:

Notes:

Name:

Address:

Home:

Mobile: Work:

Email: Fax:

Notes:

Name:

Address:

Home:

Mobile: Work:

Email: Fax:

Notes:

S

Name:

Address:

Home:

Mobile: | Work:

Email: | Fax:

Notes:

Name:

Address:

Home:

Mobile: | Work:

Email: | Fax:

Notes:

Name:

Address:

Home:

Mobile: | Work:

Email: | Fax:

Notes:

T

Name:

Address:

Home:

Mobile: | Work:

Email: | Fax:

Notes:

Name:

Address:

Home:

Mobile: | Work:

Email: | Fax:

Notes:

Name:

Address:

Home:

Mobile: | Work:

Email: | Fax:

Notes:

T

Name:

Address:

Home:

Mobile:	Work:
Email:	Fax:

Notes:

Name:

Address:

Home:

Mobile:	Work:
Email:	Fax:

Notes:

Name:

Address:

Home:

Mobile:	Work:
Email:	Fax:

Notes:

Name:

Address:

Home:

Mobile: Work:

Email: Fax:

Notes:

Name:

Address:

Home:

Mobile: Work:

Email: Fax:

Notes:

Name:

Address:

Home:

Mobile: Work:

Email: Fax:

Notes:

T

Name:

Address:

Home:

Mobile: Work:

Email: Fax:

Notes:

Name:

Address:

Home:

Mobile: Work:

Email: Fax:

Notes:

Name:

Address:

Home:

Mobile: Work:

Email: Fax:

Notes:

Name:

Address:

Home:

Mobile: Work:

Email: Fax:

Notes:

Name:

Address:

Home:

Mobile: Work:

Email: Fax:

Notes:

Name:

Address:

Home:

Mobile: Work:

Email: Fax:

Notes:

𝒰

Name:

Address:

Home:

Mobile: Work:

Email: Fax:

Notes:

Name:

Address:

Home:

Mobile: Work:

Email: Fax:

Notes:

Name:

Address:

Home:

Mobile: Work:

Email: Fax:

Notes:

Name:

Address:

Home:

Mobile: Work:

Email: Fax:

Notes:

Name:

Address:

Home:

Mobile: Work:

Email: Fax:

Notes:

Name:

Address:

Home:

Mobile: Work:

Email: Fax:

Notes:

$\mathcal{U}$

Name:

Address:

Home:

Mobile: | Work:

Email: | Fax:

Notes:

Name:

Address:

Home:

Mobile: | Work:

Email: | Fax:

Notes:

Name:

Address:

Home:

Mobile: | Work:

Email: | Fax:

Notes:

Name:

Address:

Home:

Mobile: Work:

Email: Fax:

Notes:

Name:

Address:

Home:

Mobile: Work:

Email: Fax:

Notes:

Name:

Address:

Home:

Mobile: Work:

Email: Fax:

Notes:

V

Name:

Address:

Home:

Mobile:	Work:
Email:	Fax:

Notes:

Name:

Address:

Home:

Mobile:	Work:
Email:	Fax:

Notes:

Name:

Address:

Home:

Mobile:	Work:
Email:	Fax:

Notes:

V

Name:

Address:

Home:

Mobile: | Work:

Email: | Fax:

Notes:

Name:

Address:

Home:

Mobile: | Work:

Email: | Fax:

Notes:

Name:

Address:

Home:

Mobile: | Work:

Email: | Fax:

Notes:

V

Name:

Address:

Home:

Mobile:	Work:
Email:	Fax:

Notes:

Name:

Address:

Home:

Mobile:	Work:
Email:	Fax:

Notes:

Name:

Address:

Home:

Mobile:	Work:
Email:	Fax:

Notes:

Name:

Address:

Home:

Mobile: Work:

Email: Fax:

Notes:

Name:

Address:

Home:

Mobile: Work:

Email: Fax:

Notes:

Name:

Address:

Home:

Mobile: Work:

Email: Fax:

Notes:

W

Name:

Address:

Home:

Mobile:	Work:
Email:	Fax:

Notes:

Name:

Address:

Home:

Mobile:	Work:
Email:	Fax:

Notes:

Name:

Address:

Home:

Mobile:	Work:
Email:	Fax:

Notes:

Name:

Address:

Home:

Mobile: Work:

Email: Fax:

Notes:

Name:

Address:

Home:

Mobile: Work:

Email: Fax:

Notes:

Name:

Address:

Home:

Mobile: Work:

Email: Fax:

Notes:

W

Name:

Address:

Home:

Mobile: | Work:

Email: | Fax:

Notes:

Name:

Address:

Home:

Mobile: | Work:

Email: | Fax:

Notes:

Name:

Address:

Home:

Mobile: | Work:

Email: | Fax:

Notes:

X

Name:

Address:

Home:

Mobile: Work:

Email: Fax:

Notes:

Name:

Address:

Home:

Mobile: Work:

Email: Fax:

Notes:

Name:

Address:

Home:

Mobile: Work:

Email: Fax:

Notes:

X

Name:

Address:

Home:

Mobile:	Work:
Email:	Fax:

Notes:

Name:

Address:

Home:

Mobile:	Work:
Email:	Fax:

Notes:

Name:

Address:

Home:

Mobile:	Work:
Email:	Fax:

Notes:

Name:

Address:

Home:

Mobile: | Work:

Email: | Fax:

Notes:

Name:

Address:

Home:

Mobile: | Work:

Email: | Fax:

Notes:

Name:

Address:

Home:

Mobile: | Work:

Email: | Fax:

Notes:

X

Name:

Address:

Home:

Mobile: | **Work:**

Email: | **Fax:**

Notes:

Name:

Address:

Home:

Mobile: | **Work:**

Email: | **Fax:**

Notes:

Name:

Address:

Home:

Mobile: | **Work:**

Email: | **Fax:**

Notes:

Name:

Address:

Home:

Mobile: Work:

Email: Fax:

Notes:

Name:

Address:

Home:

Mobile: Work:

Email: Fax:

Notes:

Name:

Address:

Home:

Mobile: Work:

Email: Fax:

Notes:

Y

Name:
Address:

Home:
Mobile: | Work:
Email: | Fax:
Notes:

Name:
Address:

Home:
Mobile: | Work:
Email: | Fax:
Notes:

Name:
Address:

Home:
Mobile: | Work:
Email: | Fax:
Notes:

Y

Name:

Address:

Home:

Mobile: | Work:

Email: | Fax:

Notes:

Name:

Address:

Home:

Mobile: | Work:

Email: | Fax:

Notes:

Name:

Address:

Home:

Mobile: | Work:

Email: | Fax:

Notes:

Y

Name:

Address:

Home:

Mobile: | Work:

Email: | Fax:

Notes:

Name:

Address:

Home:

Mobile: | Work:

Email: | Fax:

Notes:

Name:

Address:

Home:

Mobile: | Work:

Email: | Fax:

Notes:

Name:

Address:

Home:

Mobile: Work:

Email: Fax:

Notes:

Name:

Address:

Home:

Mobile: Work:

Email: Fax:

Notes:

Name:

Address:

Home:

Mobile: Work:

Email: Fax:

Notes:

Z

Name:

Address:

Home:

Mobile: | Work:

Email: | Fax:

Notes:

Name:

Address:

Home:

Mobile: | Work:

Email: | Fax:

Notes:

Name:

Address:

Home:

Mobile: | Work:

Email: | Fax:

Notes:

Name:

Address:

Home:

Mobile: | Work:

Email: | Fax:

Notes:

Name:

Address:

Home:

Mobile: | Work:

Email: | Fax:

Notes:

Name:

Address:

Home:

Mobile: | Work:

Email: | Fax:

Notes:

Z

Name:

Address:

Home:

Mobile: | Work:

Email: | Fax:

Notes:

Name:

Address:

Home:

Mobile: | Work:

Email: | Fax:

Notes:

Name:

Address:

Home:

Mobile: | Work:

Email: | Fax:

Notes:

Name:

Address:

Home:

Mobile: | Work:

Email: | Fax:

Notes:

Name:

Address:

Home:

Mobile: | Work:

Email: | Fax:

Notes:

Name:

Address:

Home:

Mobile: | Work:

Email: | Fax:

Notes: